The Beginning of Today: The Marihuana Tax Act of 1937

By
Kenneth Michael White

PublishAmerica
Baltimore

© 2004 by Kenneth Michael White.

All rights reserved. No part of this book may be reproduced, stored in a retrieval system or transmitted in any form or by any means without the prior written permission of the publishers, except by a reviewer who may quote brief passages in a review to be printed in a newspaper, magazine or journal.

First printing

ISBN: 1-4137-2989-4
PUBLISHED BY PUBLISHAMERICA, LLLP
www.publishamerica.com
Baltimore

Printed in the United States of America

*To all those who endure prosecution
solely for marihuana*

Acknowledgments

I would like to thank the following for their help in creating this paper: Professor Steve Hartwell, from the University of San Diego School of Law, for supporting and encouraging this effort. Professor Roy L. Brooks, from the University of San Diego School of Law, for setting the bar so high. Justice Richard Huffman, from California's bench and the University of San Diego School of Law, for affirming my faith in America's legal system. My friends who supported (and tolerated) me during the writing process. Finally, Professor Neville Cox, Lecturer in Law at Trinity College Dublin School of Law, whose combative academic nature helped sharpen my search for truth, which is the whole point after all.

Preface

Most people I speak with do not believe it should be illegal for adults to possess and use marihuana in the privacy of the home, yet few people seem to care when government resources are used to punish nonviolent marihuana users. From what I understand, marihuana is still prohibited for two reasons.
1. Fear
2. Paternalism

Marihuana prohibition exists because people are too afraid to address the issue. The Honorable Barney Frank of the House of Representatives expressly stated in a letter to the author that the end of marihuana prohibition is something that many political leaders embrace in private, but will not discuss publicly because of a fear of political retribution. Something important is lost in our politics if fear has stunted our ability to embrace intelligent social policy. To quote F.D.R., "The only thing we have to fear is fear itself."

It is also possible that people are content with the idea of paternalism—the idea that government should control what one does to one's own body. Those who embrace paternalism believe that the government should make personal decisions, or that the government is in a better position than the individual to make personal decisions. This position that *government knows best* is drastically different from the constitutionally protected right of individual liberty that practically defines what it means to be an American.

Some who argue in favor of prohibition often claim marihuana use leads to drug abuse. The argument is that the end of prohibition would result in a tidal wave of substance abuse opening up a Pandora's box that is better left alone. Considering that we have problems today suggests that prohibition doesn't work, and what is more is that there may, in fact, be nothing to fear. Hope was the final spirit to exit Pandora's box. It is possible that a more medicinal approach to the problem is better than our current law enforcement approach.

Even assuming arguendo that marihuana does currently lead to other drug use and abuse there is reason to think that this would not be so if prohibition ended. If marihuana were removed from its illegal surroundings any "gateway" effect of marihuana would likely disappear because it would no longer be sold in a market surrounded by harder drugs. In other words, the person who provides marihuana would not also provide other black-market items. Regardless, marihuana does not cause someone to do other drugs.

A negative consequence of our current marihuana policy is that industrial marihuana, which is called hemp, is artificially prohibited from the marketplace. This is the case even though hemp is very low in THC, which is the chemical in marihuana that creates the illegal intoxicating effect. Hemp cannot get a person "high." Thus, marihuana prohibition means that possibilities in paper, fabric, fuel, food, and other industrial products are lost to the market even though there is no rational basis for keeping hemp out of the stream of commerce.

Another negative consequence of our current marihuana policy is a denigration of comity between some states and the federal government. A few states have ended prohibition and legitimized medical marihuana within their boarders; however, any state law that recognizes the medicinal use of marihuana conflicts with the total prohibition of marihuana under federal law. Conflicts between federal and state laws are not good for the Union.

We, the people of the United States, are responsible for marihuana prohibition. Marihuana prohibition started with an act of Congress. They made a mistake. It happens. But since Congress rarely takes the initiative to voluntarily correct its own failings, and since it has yet to act on the matter, the people have to tell their representatives to correct the error and end marihuana prohibition. Vote.

Table Of Contents

I.	Introduction: Why Study Marihuana?	13
II.	Chapter One: America and Marihuana in 1937	15
	i. The Federal Bureau of Narcotics	16
	ii. The Role of the Media	18
	iii. The Role of Race	21
	iv. Conclusion	25
III.	Chapter Two: The Marihuana Tax Act of 1937	26
	i. The Hearings	26
	ii. The Act	29
	iii. Conclusion	30
IV.	Chapter Three: America and Marihuana Today	32
	i. The DEA	33
	ii. The Media	38
	iii. The Courts	39
	iv. Conclusion	44
V.	Table of Sources	47
VI.	Appendix	53

Author's Note:

People refer to *Cannabis sativa* in many ways with many different spellings. This book will use "marihuana," which is the traditional English spelling. When a different spelling is used in a respective source, it will be represented as it originally appeared.

Introduction: Why Study Marihuana?

Marihuana is many things. It is hemp, an industrial plant with many uses; it is farming, a traditional American way of life; it is medicine, the remedy of choice for some familiar with its properties. Marihuana is also a crime. It is a source of imprisonment; literally, a reason for incarceration, and figuratively, a habit-forming drug. Marihuana is also a plant with a net worth of billions of dollars. That fact alone justifies the study of marihuana.

Another reason we study marihuana is our interest in what is true. Boake Carter said, "In time of war the first casualty is truth." America has been at war against marihuana for 63 years. Consequently, our understanding of marihuana prohibition is the product of much conflicting, sensational, and manipulated information. This book is an attempt to find the truth beyond the cloud surrounding the debate of marihuana prohibition.

Only with open minds can we formulate a marihuana policy that will work in America. We are a land of liberty and a land of laws. Sometimes these interests conflict with each other, as they have in the case of our marihuana policy, and the result is troubling and complex. For certain, however, in the debate about which path America should choose regarding its marihuana policy, we should always remember that war is less desirable than peace.

Chapter One: America and Marihuana in 1937

"The fact is that America is now, and has always been, a nation of pill poppers. At the same time, it is a nation that prides itself on the virtues of temperance and hard work."[1] Though contradictory because it might seem odd that a person who uses drugs could also be a hard worker, these statements aptly describe America's historical relationship with marihuana. America "has both zealously embraced and vigorously outlawed the cannabis plant and its various products."[2]

In early American history marihuana was, "a cash crop, the source of the rope that rigged many of the world's sailing ships and rough fabric that covered westward-bound American pioneer wagons."[3] The paper industry used marihuana "in the manufacture of fine-grade papers, including those used in Bibles and paper currency."[4]

America's first president, George Washington, farmed marihuana. "Once, during one of his many extended absences, Washington was reported to have expressed the wistful hope that he would be able to return to his plantation in time for the September harvest."[5]

Both Thomas Jefferson and Benjamin Franklin touted the importance of marihuana to America.[6] "During pre-Revolutionary times, hemp fabric was one of the most common materials in the colonial homestead...there was virtually no household that did not contain an item made from hemp."[7]

"The Civil War discouraged the [marihuana] industry [in America] beyond all hope of resuscitation."[8] In 1931, six years before the passage of the Marihuana Tax Act of 1937 (Tax Act), the use of marihuana by minorities began to become apparent.[9] Consequently, "twenty-one states had...restricted the sale of marijuana as part of their general narcotics articles, one state had prohibited its use for any purpose, and four states had outlawed its cultivation."[10] By 1937, the year the Tax Act was passed, "nearly every state had adopted legislation outlawing marihuana."[11]

The Tax Act effectively began what is known today as "America's War on Drugs," at least with respect to marihuana. The Tax Act will be analyzed in depth in chapter two of this book. The first chapter will focus on American society at the time the Tax Act was passed. First, the role of the Federal Bureau of Narcotics in the passage of the Tax Act will be analyzed. Second, the role of the media in the passage of the Tax Act will be analyzed. Finally, the role of race in the passage of the Tax Act will be analyzed.

The Federal Bureau of Narcotics

The origin of the Federal Bureau of Narcotics (Bureau) was the passage of the Harrison Act in 1920, which criminalized the trade of opiates in America.

> Originally, the Bureau was a "division of the Prohibition Unit of the Internal Revenue Service. In 1930, the enforcement of the narcotics laws was severed from the Bureau of Prohibition and established as the separate Bureau of Narcotics in the Treasury Department. The existence of this separate agency anxious to fulfill its role as crusader against the evils of narcotics has done as much as any single factor to influence the course of drug regulation from 1930 to 1970."[12]

Speaking of the Bureau inevitably means speaking of its leader, Harry Jacob Anslinger, who reigned from 1930 to 1962. Mr. Anslinger is given credit by some for being "singlehandedly responsible for outlawing marijuana and writing the tough dope laws of today."[13] It has been said that the Tax Act "was the culmination of a series of efforts on the part of the Federal Bureau of Narcotics to generate antimarihuana legislation."[14] Even John Finlator, former Deputy Director of the Federal Bureau of Narcotics and Dangerous Drugs, credits Anslinger: "Before Harry Anslinger came along, the public didn't know anything about marijuana and they didn't care."[15]

Other critics are more tempered and do not heap all the responsibility (or blame) for America's early policy regarding marihuana on the shoulders of the Bureau and Mr. Anslinger.

"It has become quite fashionable among critics of existing marijuana legislation to assert that the sole cause of the illegal status of marijuana has been the crusading zeal of the Federal Bureau of Narcotics and especially of its long time head, Harry J. Anslinger. Some observers have suggested that the Bureau's activity was produced by bureaucratic exigencies and the need to expand; others have said the Bureau was on a moral crusade; still others have asserted that the Bureau believed its own propaganda about the link between criminality and dope fiends. While much of this may be true, it is clear that the Bureau did not single-handedly conjure up the idea of banning marijuana use. Since many states had already undertaken the regulation of marijuana before the creation of the bureau in 1930, we cannot credit the Bureau alone with the pressure to outlaw the drug."[16]

Mr. Anslinger "proudly told the story of his campaign and took credit for much of the publicity that had been given the marihuana menace."[17] The rhetoric of the publicity was that marihuana is a "killer...narcotic known to America as marijuana, and to history as hashish."[18] Mr. Anslinger said, "No one knows, when he places a marijuana cigarette to his lips, whether he will become a joyous reveler in a musical heaven, a mad insensate, a calm philosopher, or a murderer."[19]

It will likely never be definitively known whether Mr. Anslinger's representations of marihuana reflected a true concern for America's welfare, or whether they were the actions of a man set on establishing his, and his organization's, bureaucratic existence.

In 1937, a time when opiate use was common,[20] Mr. Anslinger noted that there was no connection between marihuana use and heroin, opium, or cocaine use; however, he did believe there was a connection between marihuana use and crime.[21] Mr. Anslinger held that marihuana directly caused "murders, suicides, robberies, criminal assaults, holdups, burglaries, and deeds of maniacal insanity."[22] Later, "in the Congressional hearings that led to the 1956 Narcotic Control Act, it was evident that Mr. Anslinger had drastically changed his views on the marihuana question. He played down the connection between marihuana use and crime, emphasizing instead that marihuana was dangerous primarily because it sometimes led to heroin addiction."[23] When asked if it was true that marihuana "leads many people eventually to the use of heroin, and the drugs that do cause complete addiction...Mr. Anslinger, forgetting his 1937 line [stated], 'That is the greatest problem and our great concern about the use of marihuana, that eventually, if used over a long period, it does lead to heroin addiction.'"[24]

It is significant that the justifications of marihuana prohibition offered by Mr. Anslinger changed with the times. In 1937 the reason offered for marihuana prohibition was that marihuana caused insanity and a blatant disregard for human life and health, especially in the young who were being "selected by peddlers of the poison."[25] Then, at a time when it was known that marihuana did not create criminal tendencies in people,[26] Mr. Anslinger contradicted his 1937 statements to justify the continued criminalization of marihuana in 1956. This kind of malleable representation of the nature of marihuana opens up Mr. Anslinger to charges of self-preservation and dishonesty, because "if it is true that marihuana users were not switching to heroin in 1937, it seems probable that it was the 1937 antimarihuana law itself that brought about [any alleged connection between marihuana use and heroin use]."[27]

In a 1972 government report about marihuana authorized by President Nixon, it was noted that the Bureau helped to "popularly assert that the drug brought about a large variety of social and individual ills, including crime and insanity. As a result it was prohibited by federal law in 1937."[28]

The Federal Bureau of Narcotics contributed a great deal to America's perception of marihuana as a menace in 1937. This role was intrinsically intertwined with the media and racial perceptions to produce an image of the marihuana user as an unpredictable, undesirable sociopath. When this image of the sociopath is a young, white teenage son or daughter, it becomes easier to see, perhaps, how "Congress was hoodwinked by the Federal Bureau of Narcotics" when it passed the Marihuana Tax Act of 1937.[29]

The Role of the Media

The media in 1937 had a dramatic impact on America's opinion about marihuana. "Many of the nation's newspapers were aiding the efforts of the Federal Bureau of Narcotics."[30] The Bureau used the media to conduct "an active educational campaign for federal legislation."[31] Through print and film the media gave America the details of the marihuana menace.

"Stop This Murderous Smoke," an editorial from the *Tampa Times* noted, "It may or may not be wholly true that the pernicious marihuana cigarette is responsible for the murderous mania of a Tampa young man in exterminating all the members of his family within his reach—but whether or not the poisonous mind-wrecking weed is mainly accountable for the tragedy its sale should not be and should never have been permitted here or elsewhere."[32]

The papers in New Orleans followed Tampa's lead. The *New Orleans Morning Tribune* "ran a series of articles ballyhooing the growing menace of the drug. Mostly sensationalistic in tone, the headlines blared revelations to the effect that 'SCHOOL CHILDREN FOUND IN GRIP OF MARIJUANA HABIT BY INVESTIGATORS,' 'WORKMEN OF CITY LURED BY MUGGLES ["muggles" is slang for marihuana.],' 'WELFARE WORKERS ARE POWERLESS TO COPE WITH SINISTER TRAFFIC.'"[33]

The *Chicago Herald-Examiner* reported, "A Kansas hasheesh eater thinks he is a white elephant. Six months ago they found him strolling along the road, a few miles out of Topeka. He was naked, his clothes strewn along the highway for a mile. He was not violently insane, but crazy—said he was an elephant and acted as much like one as his limited physique would let him. Marihuana did it."[34]

Perhaps the most influential reporting was of marihuana and school children. The Bureau and the media focused quite heavily on the idea that young high school children were the prey of peddlers of marihuana.[35] The *Kansas City Star*, the *Chicago Examiner*, the *Chicago-Tribune*, the *New York Times*, and the *Times-Dispatch* all took up an anti-marihuana campaign warning of the risk to American youth.[36] The *Morning Tribune* "ran a series of sensationalistic articles describing marihuana's infiltration into the city's schools."[37]

Unfortunately, the hype regarding marihuana was inaccurate. Dr. Woodward, the legislative council for the American Medical Association, noted this public deficiency of knowledge about marihuana during the hearings in which Congress considered the Tax Act.

> "You have been told that school children are great users of marihuana cigarettes. No one has been summoned from the Children's Bureau to show the nature and extent of the habit among children. Inquiry into the Office of Education, and they certainly should know something of the prevalence of the habit among school children of this country, if there is a prevalent habit, indicates that they had not occasion to investigate it and know nothing of it."[38]

In addition to newspapers and magazines, novelists seized the opportunity to promulgate the spread of the marihuana hysteria. One such author was

Morgan Robertson who published *The Poison Ship*. Robertson's novel describes how the "burning jute (New England Hemp) gives off the soporific fumes of hashish which produces drowsiness, then wild dreams and waking ecstasy."[39]

A novel by Carl Moore, *Spicy-Adventure Stories*, depicted "Scotland Yard detectives surreptiously getting a murder suspect to take some hashish. Overcome by the drug, the suspect loses consciousness, convulses, and subsequently reenacts the crime he has been arrested for (rape and murder). Convicted by the evidence, he is later hanged."[40]

Film was also used to educate America about the marihuana menace. Perhaps the most famous film on topic is *Reefer Madness*. Originally titled *The Burning Question*, the film revealed to audiences the potential horror marihuana posed to American society.

The film begins with a disclaimer: "The incidents and characters portrayed in this motion picture are purely fictional and any similarity to actual occurrences and living or deceased persons is coincidental."[41] Curiously, the next shot is of text that begs the audience to disregard the disclaimer and accept the drama about to be portrayed as true.

"The motion picture you are about to witness may startle you. It would not have been possible, otherwise, to sufficiently emphasize the frightful toll of the new drug menace which is destroying the youth of America in alarmingly increasing numbers. Marihuana is that drug—a violent narcotic—an unspeakable scourge—The Real Public Enemy Number One!

It's first effect is sudden, violent, uncontrollable laughter; then come dangerous hallucinations—space expands—time slows down, almost stands still...fixed ideas come next, conjuring up monstrous extravagances—followed by emotional disturbances, the total inability to direct thoughts, the loss of all power to resist physical emotions...leading finally to acts of shocking violence...ending often in incurable insanity. In picturing its soul-destroying effects no attempt was made to equivocate. The scenes and incidents, while fictionalized for the purpose of this story, are based upon actual research into the results of marihuana addiction. If their stark reality will make you 'think,' will make you aware that something 'must be done' to wipe out this ghastly menace, then the picture will not have failed in its purpose...

THE BEGINNING OF TODAY

> Because the dread 'Marihuana' may be reaching forth next for your son or daughter...or 'yours'...or 'YOURS!'[42]

The story of *Reefer Madness* is simple enough. Five young, white Americans are exposed to marihuana and their lives are ruined as a result. Ralph is committed to an insane asylum for life. Jimmy kills a man while driving his sister's car. He insanely screams, "I'm red-hot!" just before the accident, and right after smoking marihuana.[43] Bill is tried for murder after getting involved with marihuana. Blanch commits suicide as a result of her experiences with marihuana. Finally, Mary is killed in a marihuana den.

At the end of the film a concerned educator, known as "Dr. Carroll," comes on the screen and warns that "we must learn the truth...your daughter may end up like Ralph...or Yours!...or Yours!...or Yours!"[44]

The media, along with the Federal Bureau of Narcotics, testified to the American people and to Congress that marihuana was a menace. *But for* the drug, they said, ordinary law abiding citizens would not be murderers.[45] Somehow marihuana, the plant Thomas Jefferson grew, the plant George Washington raised at Mount Vernon, and the plant that once grew freely on the grounds where the Pentagon now stands, had been transformed from an industrial and commercial plant with recreational and medicinal purposes to a dangerous killer weed.[46] A factor in this sudden change of attitude toward marihuana was race.

The Role of Race

The attitude toward non-white races in 1937 reflected a rooted feeling of animus. This feeling helped establish the anti-marihuana myths in the American psyche and contributed to the passage of the Tax Act. The responsibility for the attitude was, in part, xenophobia. "One cannot avoid questioning to what extent cannabis is viewed, perhaps largely unconsciously, as *the* nonwhite drug which is rapidly invading the white community."[47]

The idea that a minority *plus* the use of intoxicants should *equal* the prohibition of that intoxicant began in the 1860s.[48] At that time, Chinese immigrants "poured into the American west to work on the railways that were beginning to tentacle across the country."[49] Some of these people searched for an intoxicant. They found it in opium, and "the opium den became the visible symbol of the Chinese presence on the West Coast and as such became the target of anti-Chinese sentiment."[50]

An editorial from the *Tombstone Epitaph* reveals the attitude at the time:
> The Chinese are the least desired immigrants who have ever sought the United States...the almond-eyed Mongolian with his pigtail, his heathenism, his filthy habits, his thrift, and careful accumulation of savings to be sent back to the flowery kingdom. The most we can do is to insist that he is a heathen, a devourer of soup made from the flagrant juice of the rat, filthy, disagreeable, and undesirable generally, an encumbrance that we have determined shall not increase in this part of the world.[51]

This attitude, which contributed to the criminalization of opium, set the stage for the prohibition of marihuana in 1937. In a sense, prohibition was a cultural phenomenon. "The West, with its cultural emphasis on achievement, activity, and aggressiveness, had elected alcohol as its acceptable, semiofficial euphoriant."[52] Not so in the East, however, as "cannabis has been accepted for centuries among those people...where cultural background and religious teaching support introspection, meditation, and bodily passivity."[53]

In 1937 it was mainly the attitude toward the Mexican population in the Southwest that helped create the drive to criminalize marihuana.[54] In a letter to the Bureau from the *Alamosan Daily Courier* in Alamoso, Colorado, offered into consideration at the Congressional hearings of the Tax Act, the sentiment towards the Mexican population is explained:
> The people and the officials here want to know why something can't be done about marihuana...The sheriff, district attorney, and city police are making every effort to destroy this menace. Our paper is carrying on an educational campaign to describe the weed and tell of its horrible effects...*I wish I could show you what a small marihuana cigarette can do to one of our degenerate Spanish-speaking residents.* That's why our problem is so great; the greatest percentage of our population is composed of Spanish-speaking persons, *most of whom are low mentally*, because of social and racial conditions."[55]

In an article by Dr. Frank R. Gomila, commissioner of public safety, and Miss Madeline C. Gomila, assistant city chemist, the racial bias behind the drive to prohibit marihuana is openly stated:
> "The Mexican population cultivates on average two to three tons of the weed annually. This the Mexicans make into cigarettes, which they sell at two for twenty-five cents, mostly

to white school students. We must remind friend skeptic that the great majority of indulgers are ignorant and inexperienced youngsters and *members of the lowest strata of humanity.* When you think this fact over there should be no room for argument [against marihuana prohibition]."[56]

The perceived association between violence and marihuana use by Mexicans may have its roots in the folklore of Pancho Villa, the Mexican Revolutionary hero. The soldiers of Pancho Villa reportedly smoked marihuana before going into battle.

> After getting devoutly zonked for the battle of Agua Prieta...the intrepid Indians acted like wild men completely out of their heads from inhaling marijuana. The marijuana gave them superhuman strength. So frenzied were they with the drug that some of them succeeded in breaking the wire with their hands."[57]

This legend of Pancho Villa's soldiers mirrors the story of a Persian military order called the Assassins. The Assassin myth was offered to Congress by Mr. Anslinger to justify the passage of the Tax Act.[58] Mr. Anslinger said that the Assassins "derived their name from the drug called hashish which is now known in this country as marihuana. They were noted for their acts of cruelty and the word 'assassin' very aptly describes the drug."[59]

The folksong, written in honor of Pancho Villa's victory at Torreon, sheds more light on to the connection between race and negative marihuana sentiments.

> *Well done, Pancho Villa*
> *His heart did not waver;*
> *He took the strongest fort*
> *On the hill at Torreon.*
>
> *One thing always gives me laughter*
> *Pancho Villa the morning after,*
> *Ay, there go the Carranzistras...*
> *Who comes here? The Villistas.*
>
> *Chorus:*
> *La Cucaracha, la cucaracha*

Ya no puede caminar;
Porque no tiene, porque no tiene
Marihuana que fumar.

(The cockroach, the cockroach
Can no longer walk;
Because he hasn't, because he hasn't,
Marijuana to smoke.) (High Times at 30).

Black Americans were also used as targets in the educational campaign against marihuana in 1937. The reason for this association may have stemmed from the relationship between hemp and slavery.[60] "Without hemp," writes J.F. Hopkins in his *History of the Hemp Industry in Kentucky*, "slavery might not have flourished in Kentucky since other agricultural products of the state were not conducive to the extensive use of bondsmen."[61]

In addition to slavery, jazz also contributed to the connection in the American psyche between black Americans and marihuana use. "'Moota,' as the drug was known in [New Orleans], was popular throughout the red-light district [where jazz was played by mostly black musicians], and eventually its association with this part of town came to the attention of the city's moral crusaders who began to warn of its danger to the community as a whole."[62]

"Some of the fury aroused by marihuana can be attributed to fear of that which is alien and un-American, which would make the drug seem a particularly dangerous and degenerate intoxicant."[63] America struggles to appreciate the black/white divide in civilized terms today, so it is not surprising to find that perhaps in 1937, many white Americans formed negative attitudes towards marihuana because some black Americans reportedly used it.

A blatant example of the prejudice against minorities regarding marihuana can be found in an article published in the *New Orleans Medical and Surgical Journal*:

> The debasing and baneful influence of hashish and opium is not restricted to individuals but has manifested itself in nations and races as well. The dominant race and most enlightened countries are alcoholic, whilst the races and nations addicted to hemp and opium, some of which once attained to heights of culture and civilization have deteriorated both mentally and physically.[64]

THE BEGINNING OF TODAY

Race played a significant role in forming America's policy regarding marihuana in 1937. That policy remains with us today. However, change is possible. Even though we are a nation that grew strong despite many racist policies, there are nevertheless many Americans today who now realize that the application of the words of our genesis—that all of us *are* created equal—can help us to grow even stronger. Just as our understanding of race has evolved since 1937, so too should our marihuana policy.

Conclusion

In 1937 America perceived marihuana as a plant of evil. The thinking was that users were likely to commit insane acts of violence. An extensive educational campaign warning Americans of the alleged dangers of marihuana was waged by the media with the help of the Bureau, which touched on stereotypes in the American psyche that resulted in the passage of the Tax Act.

Chapter Two: The Marihuana Tax Act of 1937

The 75th Congress, Committee on Ways and Means, heard testimony regarding the proposed Tax Act. Often times a court, to fully understand a statute at issue in a particular case, will turn to such testimony. The statute at issue in this book is the Tax Act. The following is a study of the testimony behind, and the text of, that very important law.

The Hearings

Mr. Snell. *What is the bill?*

Mr. Rayburn. *It has something to do with something that is called marihuana. I believe it is a narcotic of some kind.*

> Colloquy on the House floor prior to
> passage of the Marihuana Tax Act.[65]

On April 27, 1937, the Committee on Ways and Means discussed the proposed Marihuana Tax Act of 1937. "The brief three days of hearings on the Act present a case study in legislative carelessness."[66]

The first to speak was Mr. Hester, assistant general counsel for the Department of Treasury. He testified that marihuana was "used extensively by high school children [and] its effect is deadly."[67] Mr. Hester cited an editorial from the *Washington Herald*: "The problems of greatest menace in the U.S. seem to be the rise in use of Indian hemp (marihuana) with inadequate control laws."[68]

Mr. Hester stated the purpose of the Tax Act:

> To employ the Federal taxing power not only to raise revenue from the marihuana traffic, but also to discourage the current and widespread undesirable use of marihuana by smokers into channels where the plant will be put to valuable industrial, medicinal, and scientific uses. The proposed marihuana bill is something of a synthesis of both [The Harrison Narcotics Act] and the National Firearms Act.[69]

When asked why not just include marihuana in the existing Harrison Act, Mr. Hester explained that would not be feasible.[70] Mr. Hester said that because marihuana grew wild throughout the United States, it did not fit within the scope of the Harrison Act's prohibitions on the importation of narcotics.[71] Mr. Hester also acknowledged the industrial uses of marihuana which made the Harrison Act even less appropriate.[72] Finally, Mr. Hester revealed that there was fear about more Constitutional challenges against the Harrison Act if it was amended.[73]

Interestingly, Congress paid little attention to the question of Constitutionality during the hearings. When presented with the issue Congressman McCormack, showing little regard for notions of comity, bluntly said, "If we have the power to tax, the manner in which it is exercised is of no concern to the courts."[74]

This assured and confident attitude pervaded throughout the hearings. For instance, when congressman Reed interrupted dialogue on the floor, presumably to clarify a point, he nearly answered the question for the witness.

> I think what the Chairman wants to know is how high school children are able to get it. Is it not true that there are illicit peddlers who hang around the high school buildings, and as soon as they find out there is some boy to whom they think they can sell it, they make his acquaintance?[75]

After Mr. Hester's testimony, Mr. Anslinger spoke to the congressmen. He came to the hearings as the authority on the problem of marihuana in America. Mr. Anslinger testified: "This drug is as old as civilization itself. Homer wrote about it, as a drug which made men forget their homes, and that turned them into swine."[76]

Unfortunately for accuracy's sake, "the only two cases recorded by Homer of men forgetting their homes or being turned into swine are found in

The Odyssey, and it was not [marihuana] but the lotus that made men forget their homes. Similarly there is no indication in the only case of men being transformed into swine that [marihuana] was involved."[77]

Mr. Anslinger represented the nature of marihuana by comparing it with a rattlesnake.[78] He also said, "This drug is entirely the monster Hyde, the harmful effect of which cannot be measured. Some people will fly into a delirious rage, and they are temporarily irresponsible and may commit violent crimes."[79]

In addition to the testimony of Mr. Anslinger, congressmen heard other accounts of marihuana's harmful effects. The following is a typical example of the level of rhetoric:

> A girl student, still in her teens told a reporter she had seen some of her friends under the influence and named a boy and a girl who lost their senses so completely after smoking marihuana that they eloped and were married.[80]

There were three concerns that were presented to congressmen.[81] The first was "the seriousness of this problem as it concerns youngsters who are willing to take a chance at all times."[82] The second was "the increasing prevalence of this menace which results in a large percentage of criminal users."[83] The third concern was "the tragedy of persons who use the weed becoming unwilling offenders of the law because the central nervous system has been so affected."[84]

The dissenters to the Tax Act were few. "The only real concerns seem to have been that farmers would be inconvenienced by having to kill a plant which grew wild in many parts of the country, and that the birdseed, paint and varnish, and domestic hemp industries would be damaged by passage of the law."[85]

The sole voice of reason, in my opinion, came from Dr. Woodward who spoke as the legislative counsel for the American Medical Association.[86] Dr. Woodward offered testimony that Congress should have followed in 1937, and should follow today.

> The trouble is that we are looking on a narcotic addiction solely as a vice. It is a vice, but like all vices, it is based on human nature…Until we develop young men and young women who are able to suffer a little and exercise a certain amount of control, even though it may be inconvenient to do so, we are going to have a considerable amount of addiction to narcotics and addiction to other drugs. So that we must deal with narcotic

addiction as something more than a police measure.[87]

When presented with opposition to the Tax Act, congressmen simply responded with dismissals or insults. One advocate was treated like a child for disagreeing with the Tax Act: "Mr. Lozier, we know you, we love you, and we respect your ability as an advocate. We know that you are a real lawyer."[88]

Mr. Lozier may have been loved, but his farmer clients were not. "I know that your people are not knowingly a part or parcel of the traffic. I know that from what you say. If that is not the case, of course, they ought to come under the law, and if that is the case, they will not be hurt."[89] In other words, the government knows what's best; just do what it says.

The Tax Act hearings were an exercise in futility—the congressmen's minds were already made up prior to any testimony. As one member said, Congress was going to prevent what their "good friend [had] depicted as existing in oriental countries."[90] In doing so, however, the 75th Congress of the United States began a policy that has cost America far more than it has ever saved her.

The Act

"The Marihuana Tax Act [was] modeled directly after the earlier federal tax act regulating the opiates—the Harrison Act."[91]

The purpose of the Tax Act was "to impose an occupational excise tax [and a transfer tax] upon certain dealers in marihuana, and to safeguard the revenue therefrom by registry and recording."[92]

The Tax Act covered individuals, partnerships and their employees and officers, trusts, associations, companies, and corporations.[93] It defined marihuana as many things, and it covered "all parts of the plant Cannabis sativa L., whether growing or not."[94] The parameters of the act were "every compound, manufacture, salt, derivative, mixture, or preparation of [the] plant, its seeds, or resin."[95]

All transactions involving marihuana were within the scope of the act. Importers, producers, manufacturers, and even people who gave the plant away were required to pay a federal tax.[96] The amount of the tax depended upon the nature of the transaction involved.[97] For example, "Importers, manufacturers, and compounders of marihuana [had to pay] $24 per year."[98] Others, such as physicians, dentists, and veterinary surgeons only paid $1 per year.[99]

The Tax Act required "any person not a physician, dentist, veterinary surgeon, or other practitioner...to register his name or style and his place or places of business with the collector of the district in which such place or places of business are located."[100] Those persons who registered with the federal government could "deal in, dispense, or give away marihuana imported, manufactured, compounded, or produced...without further payment of the tax."[101] Conversely, those who did not register were required to pay a tax for each transaction involving marihuana.[102] If no tax was paid, an offense occurred which invoked the police measures of the Tax Act.[103]

If marihuana was found on a person's land, that person was presumed to have been a producer of marihuana and would be subject to the penalties of the Tax Act.[104] This created a burden on people to eradicate any wild growing marihuana from their property.

A concomitant effect of the Tax Act was bureaucratic red tape. Section 5(c) required the creation of "suitable forms to be prepared [for transactions involving marihuana]."[105] These forms were to be preserved for "a period of two years so as to be readily accessible for inspection by any [authorized] officer, agent, or employee."[106]

Perhaps the harshest effect of the Tax Act was on the casual user of marihuana. After the Tax Act, the jazz clubs of New Orleans were no longer filled with marihuana smoke, or if they were it was probably illegal marihuana smoke because any person who dealt with marihuana, but did not pay the special tax, had to pay $100 per ounce of marihuana.[107] In 1937, in a less than booming economy, there were probably few people that paid such a high tax. Not paying the tax, however, was an unlawful act.

The penalty for violating the Tax Act was a "fine of not more than $2,000 and/or imprisonment for not more than five years for violation of each provision of the Act."[108] Interestingly, compared to some earlier state laws, this penalty is considerably lenient. At one time, for example, "in Louisiana a 21-year-old man who [was] caught giving some pot to his 20-year-old girlfriend [could've been] legally executed."[109]

Conclusion

The Tax Act did many things. Simply put, it imposed a tax on marihuana. More significantly, "by making the individual who wished to smoke marihuana pay $100 tax per ounce, the government would effectively force the user to purchase it in an underground market, thereby exposing himself to the risk of tax evasion."[110] After the passage of the Tax Act, law enforcement increased in an area inappropriate for total scrutiny, while our individual liberties and personal freedoms shrank.

Chapter Three: America and Marihuana Today

The policy of criminalizing marihuana, which began in 1937 with the passage of the Tax Act, continues to this day. "In 1996, 641,642 Americans were arrested for marijuana offenses; that's approximately one arrest every 49 seconds. About 85% of those were for simple possession—not manufacture or distribution."[111]

Despite the mostly innocuous nature of marihuana[112] the policy of criminalization shows no signs of ending. "In 1969, $65 million was spent by the Nixon administration on the drug war [which includes more than just marihuana]; in 1982 the Reagan administration spent $1.65 billion; and in 1998 the Clinton administration requested $17.1 billion."[113]

Today, speaking of the war against marihuana means speaking of the general war on drugs, which identifies more than just marihuana as an enemy. All the money spent on fighting the war on drugs is designed to prevent harm to "our children and the poor."[114] However, "despite the fact that federal spending on the drug war increased from $1.65 billion in 1982 to $13.25 billion in 1995, about half of the students in the United States in 1995 tried an illegal drug before they graduated from high school."[115] Furthermore, even though "The Office of National Drug Control Policy says its top priority is trying to save kids from using drugs, [it] only plans to use…11.8% of its fiscal year 1999 Federal Drug Control budget to reduce youth drug use. This number includes funding to 'support and disseminate scientific research and data on the consequences of legalizing drugs,' and the creation of partnerships with the media and the entertainment industry."[116]

The actual result of the war on drugs is that "The United States operates the biggest prison system on the planet."[117] "The overall U.S. incarceration rate is six times that of its nearest Western competitors."[118]

Ironically, the effect of the war on drugs harms America's youth—the very group we are trying to protect. The most obvious harm is that there is less money for education. "From 1984 to 1996, California built 21 new prisons, and only one new university."[119] Furthermore, "California state government expenditures on prisons increased 30% from 1987 to 1995, while spending on higher education decreased by 18%."[120]

In addition to less money for educational needs, American youth also suffer from a chilling effect as a result of the war against marihuana.

> A final cost of the possession laws is the disrespect which the laws and their enforcement engender in the young. Our youth cannot understand why society chooses to criminalize a behavior with so little visible ill-effects or adverse social impact, particularly when so many members of the law enforcement community also question the same laws. These young people have jumped the fence and found no cliff. And the disrespect for the possession laws fosters a disrespect for all law and the system in general.[121]

America should adjust its marihuana policy in degree. Total prohibition should only be pursued when absolutely necessary, and even then great caution should be exercised. Extremism generally makes poor public policy; in the case of marihuana, the federal government's policy of total prohibition is too much. The National Commission on Marihuana and Drug Abuse agrees. "The actual and potential harm of [marihuana] is not great enough to justify intrusion by the criminal law into private behavior, a step which our society takes only with the greatest reluctance."[122]

This chapter will explore America's current war against marihuana, first by looking at the Drug Enforcement Administration (DEA), then the media, and finally the courts.

The DEA

The DEA is today's equivalent to the Bureau. I cannot help but wonder if the same concerns for self-preservation, present in an analysis about the Bureau, exist in an analysis of the DEA. The DEA, like the Bureau before it, assures America that is not the case. The DEA holds that its "vested interest in enforcing the drug laws of the United States"[123] is not a factor in its vigorous opposition to any reform of marihuana policy. It has the burden to prove this is true.

The position of the DEA is that the war on drugs is necessary because drugs have "devastating consequences for our entire nation."[124] While this may be true, that does not mean *ipso facto* that criminalization is the best policy for a free society because "the use of drugs is not in itself an irresponsible act."[125]

The DEA claims that the only opposition to today's drug policy is "affluent, well-educated and socially distant" individuals from the "Upper East side of New York, country clubs on both coasts of the nation, and in locations remote from the realities of drug addiction, despair and the social decay that accompany drug use."[126] First, not all opponents to the war on drugs are rich. I am quite sure that the poor man serving time for possession disagrees with the war on drugs. Second, if the opposition to the war on drugs *is* coming from educated minds, then shouldn't America, as an enlightened nation, pay heed to its educated members?

The DEA also argues "drug supply drives demand."[127] This is not the case in the Netherlands, however, which has decriminalized marihuana. In the Netherlands the prevalence of marihuana use by adolescents is 11% compared to 18% here in the United States.[128]

The DEA also argues "the enforcement of drug laws has had a significant impact on reducing the crime rate."[129] Again, in the Netherlands the homicide rate per 100,000 people is 1.8 as compared to 8 here in the United States.[130]

Just because the liberal Dutch have experienced success with decriminalization, however, is not a sufficient reason by itself to justify decriminalization here in the United States—though it is another weight on the scale that is, in my opinion, tipped in favor of ending the war against marihuana.

The DEA poses a number of questions "to ask legalization advocates…[which it believes] cannot be answered adequately."[131] As an advocate for peace in this matter, I will attempt to answer the DEA's questions.

Will all drugs be legalized?

No. I do not believe that the end of today's war on drugs means that all drugs will be freely available—just controlled in a better fashion than they currently are, without the huge societal cost of choosing incarceration over education. The point is to address each drug individually, and make a rational policy determination regarding each drug. Marihuana is a drug whose nature "does not constitute a public health problem of any significant dimensions. It is, for instance, far more innocuous in terms of physiological and social damage than alcohol or tobacco."[132] We should treat marihuana in a similar manner as we treat alcohol and tobacco.[133]

How do we address the black market that will inevitably spring up to provide newer, purer, more potent drugs to those now addicted who cannot be satisfied with the product they obtain from the government or the private sector?

Ironically, it is the current policy that has created a black market that harms America today. It harms her because the black market is an unregulated and uncontrolled source of drugs for anybody, including children. At least with regulation, access to marihuana can be controlled—not in a perfect way, of course, because everything we do is subject to our imperfect taint; however, access to marihuana could be better controlled than it is today.

This question also assumes that a regulatory scheme of marihuana prohibition could not function with change, an idea that is quite contradictory to notions of a free market.

Given the fact that our record with cigarettes and alcohol is not very good, how will we limit the abundance of dangerous drugs to 18 or 21 year olds?

Our record with cigarettes and alcohol is not very good, I agree, and I wonder why we do not do more regarding them, including limiting their access to our nation's youth via advertising and sponsorship. However, just because peace will be difficult that is not reason enough to continue a war. There are things America can do to curb drug use, and to raise the kind of children Dr. Woodward referred to above, if she is willing. In my mind, the best thing America can do regarding its youth, in a policy sense, is to choose education over the criminal law whenever possible.

Regarding adults, America can change its *mens rea* requirement for *malum in se* crimes so that a plea of "intoxication shall not be a defense to any criminal act committed under [the] influence [of drugs], nor shall proof of such intoxication constitute a negation of specific intent."[134] I would include alcohol in this policy change too. This would be an improvement over our current policy because it would be a sure signal that America does not tolerate irresponsible drug or alcohol use. Those who use drugs or alcohol and commit acts of violence in society should be punished, yet those who simply use drugs or alcohol should not.

Who will pay for the health costs and social costs which will accrue as a result of increased drug use?

First, it is not known with certainty that the decriminalization of marihuana will result in an increased use of marihuana. The situation in the Netherlands, which has decriminalized marihuana, suggests that under a regulatory scheme less people might actually use marihuana.[135] Second, decriminalization of marihuana could increase state revenue. In California, which has a billion dollar agricultural industry, marihuana is the biggest cash crop, yet the state receives no benefit from its trade.[136] Third, this question touches on a problem beyond marihuana—the lack of affordable health care in America. Perhaps the billions of dollars saved by ending the war on drugs would be enough to implement a system of health care and education whose benefits would far exceed those of our current policy.

Whose taxes will pay for the thousands of babies born drug-addicted?

Most of the concerns in this area are not marihuana related. "Epidemiological studies have found no evident link between prenatal use of marijuana and birth defects in humans."[137]

Speaking more broadly, "criminalizing substance abuse during pregnancy discourages substance-using or abusing women from seeking prenatal care, drug treatment, and other social services, and sometimes leads to unnecessary abortions."[138] Furthermore, the problem may seem worse than it is, for when "presented with children randomly labeled 'prenatally cocaine exposed' and 'normal,' childcare professionals ranked the performance of the 'prenatally cocaine-exposed' children below that of 'normal,' despite actual performance."[139]

THE BEGINNING OF TODAY

What responsibility will our society have to these children as they grow and have problems as a result of their drug use?

America owes all of its children the same duty of care. There are drug-addicted babies born under the current policy and there will be drug-addicted babies born under a different policy. By taking the important steps regarding America's overall health care problem, these concerns of drug-addicted babies can be competently addressed. I must reveal my faith that in a system where the realities of drug use are taught to our citizens and our children in effective ways, there will be less drug use and, therefore, less drug-addicted babies.

Will drug centers be located in the inner cities, or will drug distribution centers be set up in the suburbs?

This question touches on a problem that communities have dealt with in the past. The question is, where should a moral and free society geographically permit the use of vices? Some communities have answered this question by concentrating all the vices in one area. Other communities have answered this question by spreading out the vice throughout the community. The point is that this question should not be answered at the federal level, but instead at the local level.

And most legalization experts cannot answer this question: Can we set up a legalization pilot program in your neighborhood?

I would welcome a "legalization pilot program" in my neighborhood provided it had sufficient safeguards against abuse. First, there must be treatment centers where citizens can get counseling and information. Second, there must be a vigorous and sincere educational effort. Finally, proprietors of the intoxication trade should realize that the improper sale of an intoxicant will be severely punished, and users of intoxicants should understand the harsh consequences for criminal behavior while intoxicated—hence law enforcement still has a role in a non-criminalization scheme.

In sum, the DEA admits "we have not yet effectively addressed all of the drug problems facing our nation today."[140] Yet the DEA equates the end of the war on drugs with "surrender."[141] That is not my position. On the contrary, I believe the end of the war on drugs is the first step to victory.

The DEA notes "everything we've done [and continue to do] to date to find a cure for cancer—even though we have spent billions of dollars on research and we have not yet found a cure."[142] In other words, just because the billions of dollars that America spends on the war on drugs has not eliminated drug use, that does not mean we should not continue to spend billions of dollars on the war because one day it might end drug use. The DEA takes this position even though people and intoxication have been together since the beginning.[143]

I think there is a better way to spend America's money. America's other problems identified by the DEA in Congressional Hearings, "AIDS, declining educational standards, [and] homelessness," could all benefit from the resources currently channeled into an ineffective war.

The DEA has not, in my opinion, met its burden of proving that it is fundamentally concerned with more than its own budgetary existence. The DEA's embrace of a policy that began with misinformation, hypocrisy, and racial stereotypes makes it a suspect agency with suspect motives.

The Media

Today's media is quite different from the one in 1937, at least with respect to its position on marihuana. Today's media, generally, represents both sides of the marihuana issue. It may still be open to charges of sensationalism, but that is more due to its nature than any agenda against marihuana.

Today, the headlines on marihuana run the gamut.[144] Politicians even make headlines rallying against the status quo. "New Mexico Gov. Gary Johnson is now the highest elected official to advocate the legalization of drugs. Johnson said everything from marijuana to heroin ought to be legalized because he believes the U.S. anti-drug effort is an expensive bust."[145] The governor expanded on his ideas by saying, "Marijuana is the best candidate to be legalized first, followed by more dangerous drugs such as heroin—or cocaine…[but] I don't want to see it in grocery stores. I'm assuming that wouldn't happen. The more dangerous the perception of the drug, the more control there would be."[146]

Not all of today's reports, however, place marihuana in a positive light. In June 21, 2000, a report noted, "Marijuana may be greater cancer risk than tobacco."[147] The report concluded, "What we already know about marijuana smoke, coupled with our new finding that THC may encourage tumor growth, suggests that regular use of marijuana may increase the risk of respirator-tract cancer and further studies will be needed to evaluate this possibility."[148]

Unlike the media in 1937, today's media will print more than the government's position regarding marihuana. For example, in September 17, 2000, CNN reported, "The problem is overuse of anything. It can be sports, it can be television, it can be video games. Moderation is the key."[149]

Other reports recognize a distinction between marihuana use by adults vs. children:

> I do think we all need to make the distinction that when we talk about stopping the arrest of marijuana smokers, we're talking about adults smoking marijuana in the privacy of their own home. We're not advocating that it should be legal to smoke in the park, and we certainly don't think marijuana is for kids.[150]

Popular magazines and television have even taken up the marihuana issue. In a price comparison analysis, *Mountain Bike* notes that the price per pound of marihuana is $750, while the price per pound of a 1999 Porsche is $30.07. *Mountain Bike* then notes that the price "of getting caught with a pound of pot in the trunk of your Porsche, in years [is] 1 to 4."[151]

Television uses marihuana to get laughs or advertise a ware. *The Simpson's* and *That 70's Show* are two sitcoms that have parodied the criminalization of marihuana. (Fox). Sprint PCS, a wireless phone company, uses the familiar scene of a politician's shameful admission of smoking marihuana at a press conference to sell its product.[152]

In sum, the media today is generally neutral when it comes to marihuana. The reporting presents both sides of the issue with little or no detectable bias (although some media outlets do negatively refer to marihuana as "pot," which does imply some bias). However, in contrast to the media in 1937, today's media is not at fault, except in a historical sense, for America's current policy regarding marihuana.

The Courts

On the whole, America's courts have responded to the criminalization of marihuana with commendable restraint. Unfortunately, this restraint played a major role in the facilitation of America's War on Drugs. America's courts have faced serious constitutional questions as a result of the policies of the war on drugs.[153] The courts have generally recognized the constitutional authority to maintain marihuana prohibition; however, some courts have questioned the authority of the government to completely prohibit marihuana from society.

> "In *People v. Sinclair*, Justice T.G. Kavanaguh, [in a concurring opinion], rested his opinion squarely on the basic right of the individual to be free from government intrusions. He found the marijuana possession statute to be 'an impermissible intrusion on the fundamental rights to liberty and the pursuit of happiness, and is an unwarranted interference with the right to possess and use private property.' He noted the basic freedom of the individual to be free to do as he pleases so long as his actions do not interfere with the rights of his neighbor or of society. 'Big Brother' cannot, in the name of *Public* health, dictate to anyone what he can eat or drink or smoke in the *privacy* of his own home.'"[154]

Despite the above precedent, the court in *Ravin* still ruled against the individual in favor of the state's criminalization of marihuana.[155] In support of its holding, the court noted the importance of the state's interest in keeping intoxicated drivers off its highways.[156]

Petitioners have sought to challenge the statutes that criminalize marihuana in many ways. Their burden is quite difficult, however, as one court points out:

> "A statute is presumed to be constitutional. The party attacking the statute must show with convincing clarity that the statute is unconstitutional. Assuming that it can be shown that the legislature has enacted legislation on the basis of fear induced hysteria, such proof does not relieve the party attacking the statute of the burden of clearly showing that no rational factual basis exists to support the statute."[157]

It is the rational relation test—a relatively easy standard to meet—that stands in the way of those seeking redress in the courts regarding marihuana. In my opinion, that is a good thing. The policy of marihuana criminalization began in the legislature—an elected branch of our government. In other words, it was the people who enacted the criminalization of marihuana. Therefore, it is the people who must rescind that policy, not the courts. When courts rule against an otherwise constitutional statute on the basis that it is unwise, the courts have over-stepped their constitutional authority and compromised the precious system of checks and balances that is so important to our government.[158]

There is no shortage of case law regarding marihuana.[159] Interestingly, not all of it is in accord with each other. In the wake of state initiatives authorizing the medical use of marihuana, courts have struggled.[160]

America's policy regarding marihuana has had a significant impact on many facets of our Constitution. In *Draper v. United States*, the Supreme Court upheld the conviction of a person who was arrested without a warrant based on predictive detail received from a paid informant. What was the predictive detail? The petitioner "start[ed] walking 'fast' toward the exit [of a train station]."[161] This led to the petitioner's arrest and subsequent conviction when the police stopped the petitioner and found narcotics on his person. This precedent furthers the needs of law enforcement for sure; however, the cost is that walking fast in an airport or train station can give rise to probable cause based on nothing more than paid testimony.

In *Illinois v. Gates*, the Supreme Court extended its holding in *Draper* to allow a partially corroborated anonymous informant's tip to justify the issuance of a warrant based on probable cause.[162] Despite the fact that *Draper* involved a *known* paid informant, the Supreme Court nevertheless held in *Illinois v. Gates* that innocent activity—in this case traveling by car on our nation's highways—can give rise to a finding of probable cause based on nothing more than predictive detail received from an *anonymous* tipster.[163]

In *Florida v. Bostick*, the Supreme Court sanctioned intrusive police conduct and vindicated the war on drugs at the expense of the traveling American citizen. Writing for the majority, Justice O'Connor described the current state of our fundamental right to travel:

> Drug interdiction efforts have led to the use of police surveillance at airports, train stations, and bus depots. Law enforcement officers stationed at such locations routinely approach individuals, either randomly or because they suspect in some vague way that the individuals may be engaged in criminal activity, and ask them potentially incriminating questions. Broward County has adopted such a program. County Sheriff's Department officers routinely board buses at scheduled stops and ask passengers for permission to search their luggage.[164]

The facts of *Florida v. Bostick* reveal a state of affairs that runs counter to the constitutional right to travel.

> Two officers, complete with badges, insignia and one of them holding a recognizable zipper pouch, *containing a pistol*, boarded a bus bound from Miami to Atlanta during a stopover in Fort Lauderdale. Eyeing the passengers, the officers *admittedly without articulable suspicion*, picked out the defendant passenger and asked to inspect his ticket and identification. The ticket, from Miami to Atlanta, matched the defendant's identification and both were immediately returned to him as unremarkable. However, the two police officers persisted and explained their presence as narcotics agents on the lookout for illegal drugs. In pursuit of that aim, they then requested the defendant's consent to search his luggage. Needless to say, there is a conflict in the evidence about whether the defendant consented to the search of the second bag in which the contraband was found and as to whether he was informed of his right to refuse consent. However, any conflict must be resolved in favor of the state, it being a question of fact decided by the trial judge.[165]

The dissent in *Florida v. Bostick* noted that there is a "new and increasingly common tactic in the war on drugs: the suspicionless police sweep of buses in interstate or intrastate travel."[166] The dissent also noted "these sweeps are conducted in 'dragnet' style…Never do the officers advise the passengers that they are free not to speak with the officers…To put it mildly, these sweeps are inconvenient, intrusive, and intimidating."[167]

In my own opinion, an intrusive and intimidating search lacking an articulable fact or probable cause is contrary to a free nation and the 4th Amendment's guarantee against unreasonable searches and seizures.

In *Rochin v. California*, police efforts in the war on drugs increased in scope.

> Having 'some information that [the petitioner] was selling narcotics,' three deputy sheriffs of the County of Los Angeles, on the morning of July 1, 1949, made for the two-story dwelling house in which Rochin lived with his mother, common-law wife, brothers and sisters. Finding the outside door open, they [illegally] entered and then forced open the door to Rochin's room on the second floor. Inside they found petitioner sitting partly dressed on the side of the bed, upon which his wife was

lying. On a 'night-stand' beside the bed the deputies spied two capsules. When asked 'Whose stuff is this?' Rochin seized the capsules and put them in his mouth. A struggle ensued, in the course of which the three officers 'jumped upon him' and attempted to extract the capsules. The force they applied proved unavailing against Rochin's resistance. He was handcuffed and taken to a hospital. At the direction of one of the officers a doctor forced an emetic solution through a tube in Rochin's stomach against his will. This 'stomach pumping' produced vomiting. In the vomited matter were found two capsules which proved to contain morphine.[168]

Fortunately, the Supreme Court declined to sanction this kind of police behavior. The court held that such police conduct violates the Substantive Due Process Clause of the 14th Amendment of the United States Constitution because it "shocks the conscious."[169]

However, any respite from the excessive police conduct described in *Rochin* has been short. The court in *State v. Thompson* "held that the use of a choke hold ('lateral vascular neck restraint') that rendered a person unconscious for about ten seconds, in order to extract narcotic substances 'between the size of a pinhead and a pea' from his mouth, was not an unreasonable search or otherwise unconstitutional."[170]

In addition to individual liberty, the war on drugs has also impacted the right to own property.

The Drug Abuse Prevention and Control Act provides for a civil forfeiture proceeding in rem. 21 U.S.C. §881 (Supp. 1996). Upon proof that the property is used in an illegal drug transaction, the property itself is forfeited, except for any interest in an innocent owner. The act also provides for criminal forfeiture of property by a person convicted of illegal drug activity (id. §853). Each element of the criminal offense must be proved beyond a reasonable doubt. Criminal forfeiture is in personam; it is imposed as a punishment and only the defendant's interest in the property is forfeited. The federal RICO statute also provides for criminal forfeiture of property used in dealing in drugs or acquired with funds from the activity. 18 U.S.C. §1963 (Supp. 1996).[171]

Obviously, our courts have utilized much of their finite resources to adjudicate issues that arise from America's War on Drugs. Not only are our individual liberties and property rights threatened as a result of America's drug laws, but the important policy of judicial economy is compromised as well. Regarding marihuana, this expenditure of court resources directly flows from the passage of the Tax Act and it is not necessary. We should not base our current marihuana policy on the thinking of 1937.

Conclusion

In a way, the situation of marihuana today is similar to the situation of marihuana in 1937—both societies criminalized marihuana. But in another way, the situation is different. In 1937, the penalty for possession was money. Today, mere possession of marihuana can lead to prison.[172]

Another marked difference between America today and America in 1937 is the amount of information available to the public. Today, the evidence shows marihuana to be, on the whole, innocuous.[173] Its use and effect is similar to that of tobacco and alcohol.[174] This begs the question, why is marihuana still completely prohibited? Some have pointed to cultural factors, while others believe in grand conspiracies involving the oil, cotton, paper, and alcohol industries.

Marihuana is prohibited for many reasons—one of which is the stigma that surrounds the plant. It is not easy to speak against marihuana prohibition because it means speaking against a rooted history of disapproval. It means being subjected to stereotypes, discrimination, and charges of child endangerment. Hence, the professional sector of America, the middle, keeps silent about marihuana because it is easy and safe to do so.

President Clinton encountered the stereotype against marihuana, and he became the butt of many jokes with his claim that he tried marihuana as a youth, but did not inhale. The obvious lie reveals President Clinton's desire not to look the fool. It also reveals that marihuana is everywhere in America today—even in the office of the President. Yet, we continue to avoid addressing the marihuana issue.

No one should suffer the criminal justice system solely for marihuana. I say this because I believe in the sovereignty of the individual as explained by John Stuart Mill.[175] In America, one of our great treasures is the pursuit of happiness. This pursuit must be followed according to each individual's own conscious. When it comes to the issue of experiencing an intoxicant in a non-violent fashion, the government is out of its constitutional domain of authority.

This does not mean that America should totally recant its marihuana policy and encourage marihuana use. An intoxicated citizen is not the best citizen, and the United States need not encourage poor citizenry; however, taking marihuana out of the criminal justice system does not mean, by itself, that America encourages the use of marihuana. The difference is *decriminalization* instead of *legalization*. The semantic distinction is important. In a regulatory scheme of decriminalization, America could take an anti-marihuana stance. That stance would likely be more successful than today's anti-marihuana campaign because it could be based on reality. Our current policy does not allow America to disseminate all the truth regarding marihuana, because to teach that would surely be to teach the end of the war against marihuana.

Table of Sources

Abel, Ernest, L., *Marihuana The First Twelve Thousand Years*, (1980).
Albo v. State, 379 So 2d 648, (1980).
Allam v. State, 830 P2d 435, (1992).
Anslinger, Harry, J., *Marihuana: Assassin of Youth*, (1937).
Arredondo v. State, 324 SW2d 217, (1959).
Blincoe v. State, 231 Ga 886, (1974).
Bonnie, Richard, J., & Whitebread, Charles, II., *The Forbidden Fruit and the Tree of Knowledge: An Inquiry into the Legal History of American Marijuana Prohibition*, 56 Virginia Law Review 971, (1970).
Borras v. State, 229 So 2d 244, (1969).
Brantley v. State, 548 P2d 675, (1976).
Broom v. State, 463 SW2d 220, (1970).
Cain v. State, 830 P2d 435, (1990).
Cavaness v. State, 581 P2d 475, (1978).
(CNN), Cable News Network, "Bel Air pot grower sentenced to prison," (2000).
(CNN), Cable News Network, "California Could Legalize Pot in Bumper Crop of Propositions," (1996).
(CNN), Cable News Network, "California OK's Marijuana For Medicinal Use," (1996).
(CNN), Cable News Network, "Clinton may oppose medical use of illicit drugs," (1996).
(CNN), Cable News Network, "Hawaii governor signs medical marijuana bill," (2000).
(CNN), Cable News Network, "Law enforcement officials fear marijuana law fallout," (1996).
(CNN), Cable News Network, "Drug Crazy," (1999).
(CNN), Cable News Network, "Links found between marijuana and vision," (1999).
(CNN), Cable News Network, "Maine sheriff proposes seized pot be used for medicinal purposes," (2000).

(CNN), Cable News Network, "Marijuana proponents relish victory," (1996).

(CNN), Cable News Network, "Medical marijuana grower slapped with stiff sentence," (1999).

(CNN), Cable News Network, "Medical marijuana rules criticized," (1999).

(CNN), Cable News Network, "Mexico making headway in war against drugs," (1996).

(CNN), Cable News Network, "Multination drug sweep nets 2,331 arrests," (2000).

(CNN), Cable News Network, "No Deal on Medical marijuana," (1997).

(CNN), Cable News Network, "Republicans, White House unite to fight new drug laws," (1996).

(CNN), Cable News Network, "San Francisco club raid re-ignites conflict over legalized marijuana," (1997).

(CNN), Cable News Network, "Saying No To Drugs," (1996).

(CNN), Cable News Network, "Singing the praises of pot on 'Hempilation 2,'" (1998).

(CNN), Cable News Network, "Study casts doubt on marijuana's effectiveness as glaucoma treatment," (1998).

(CNN), Cable News Network, "Survey of teens shows reduction of drug use," (1998).

(CNN), Cable News Network, "Teen-age drug use down, anti-drug group's survey finds," (1999).

(CNN), Cable News Network, "Toward Legalization?" (1996).

(CNN), Cable News Network, "Weed Wars," (1996).

Comment, *Marijuana Possession and the California Constitutional Prohibition of Cruel or Unusual Punishment*, 21 UCLA L Rev. 1136, (1974).

Comment, *Ravin v. State: A Case for Privacy and Possession of Pot*, 5 UCLA-Alaska L Rev 178, (1975).

Commonwealth v. Leis, 243 NE2d 898, (1969).

Crow v. State, 551 P2d 279, (1976).

Cuevas v. State, 279 So 2d 817, (1969).

DEA Congressional Testimony, Before the Subcommittee on Criminal Justice, Drug Policy and Human Resources, Constantine, Thomas, A., (1999).

Dickerson v. State, 414 So 2d 998, (1982).

Draper v. United States, 358 U.S. 307, (1959).

Drug War Facts, Wright, Kendra, E., & Lewin, Paul, M., (1998).
Dukeminier, Jesse, and Krier, James, E., *Property*, 4th Ed., (1998).
Florida v. Bostick, 501 U.S. 429, (1991).
Fox programming, (2000).
Fotianos v. State, 329 So 2d 397, (1976).
Grinspoon, Lester, M.D., *Marihuana Reconsidered*, 2nd Edition, (1971).
Griswold v. Connecticut, 381 U.S. 479 (1965).
Hamilton v. State, 366 So 2d 8, (1978).
Haynes v. State, 312 So 2d 406, (1975).
High Times Greatest Hits, (1994).
Homer, *The Odyssey*.
Humanity, 48 Notre Dame Lawyer 314, (1972).
Huffman, Richard, Justice, Professor, University of San Diego School of Law. 5998 Alcala Park, San Diego, CA 92110.
Illinois v. Gates, 462 U.S. 213, (1983).
Illinois Norml, Inc. v. Scott, 66 Ill App 3d 633, (1978).
Kreisher v. State, 319 A2d 31, (1974).
Laird v. State, 342 So 2d 962, (1977).
Maisler v. State, 425 So 2d 107, (1982).
Marcoux v. Atty. Gen., 375 NE2d 688, (1978).
Marihuana Tax Act of 1937, United States Statutes at Large, Volume 50, Part One, (1937).
Martinez v. State, 373 SW2d 246, (1963).
Miller v. State, 458 SW2d 680, (1970).
Mountain Bike, November, (1999).
National Commission on Marihuana and Drug Abuse, *Marihuana: A signal of misunderstanding*, (1972).
People v. Aguiar, 257 Cal App. 2d 597, (1968).
People v. Bloom, 270 Cal App 2d 731, (1969).
People v. Brisco, 78 Ill App 3d 282, (1979).
People v. Campbell, 16 Ill App 3d 851, (1974).
People v. Downing, 37 Ill App 3d 297, (1976).
People v. Fillhart, 403 NYS2d 642, (1978).
People v. Foster, 260 Cal App 2d 84, (1968).
People v. Glaser, 238 Cal App 2d 819, (1965).
People v. Hesse, 18 Ill App 3d 669, (1974).
People v. Irvin, 264 Cal App 2d 747, (1968).
People v. Kline, 16 Ill App 3d 1017, (1974).

People v. Mayberry, 63 Ill App 2d 1, (1976).
People v. McCaffrey, 29 Ill App 3d 1088, (1975).
People v. McKenzie, 458 P2d 232, (1969).
People v. Nissen, 412 NYS2d 999, (1979).
People v. Normand, 440 P2d 282, (1968).
People v. Oatis, 264 Cal App 2d 324, (1968).
People v. Oliver, 66 Cal App 2d 431, (1944).
People v. Pearson, 403 NW2d 498, (1987).
People v. Perez, 289 NYS2d 450, (1967).
People v. Rhoades, 74 Ill App 3d 247, (1979).
People v. Riddle, 237 NW2d 491, (1975).
People v. Shackelford, 379 NW2d 487, (1985).
People v. Sinclair, 194 NW2d 878, (1972).
People v. Tharp, 272 Cal App 2d 268, (1969).
People v. Trippet, 56 Cal App 4th 1532, (1997).
People v. Velasquez, 666 P2d 567, (1983).
People v. Waxman, 199 NW2d 884, (1972).
People v. Widener, 220 Cal App 2d 826, (1963).
People v. Williams, 355 NW2d 268, (1984).
People v. Young, 361 NYS2d 762, (1974).
Ravin v. State, 537 P2d 494, (1975).
Reefer Madness (*The Burning Question*), film, Dezel, Albert Productions, (1936)
Rochin v. California, 342 U.S. 165, (1952).
Soler, *Of Cannabis and the Courts: A Critical Examination of Constitution Challenges to Statutory Marijuana Prohibitions*, 6 Conn L Rev. 601, (1974).
Solomon, David, *The Marihuana Papers*, (1966).
SPRINT TV Advertisement, (2000)
State v. Anderson, 558 P2d 307, (1976).
State v. Baker, 56 Hawaii 271, (1975).
State v. Beck, 329 A2d 190, (1974).
State v. Bonoa, 136 So 15, (1931).
State v. Chrisman, 364 So 2d 906, (1978).
State v. Dickamore, 592 P2d 681, (1979).
State ex rel. Scott v. Conaty, 187 SE2d 119, (1972).
State v. Gerry, 595 P2d 49, (1979).
State v. Harian, 556 So 2d 256, (1990).

State v. Infante, 260 NW2d 323, (1977).
State v. Kantner, 53 Hawaii 327, (1972).
State v. Kaplan, 209 se2D 325, (1974).
State v. Kells, 259 NW2d 19, (1977).
State v. Kelly, 106 Idaho 268, (1984).
State v. Kincaid, 98 Idaho 440, (1977).
State v. Lange, 529 NW2d 615, (1994).
State v. Leins, 234 NW2d 645, (1975).
State v. McBride, 24 Kan. App 2d 909, (1998).
State v. Murphy, 570 P2d 1070, (1977).
State v. Neal, 191 NW2d 458, (1971).
State v. Nugent, 312 a2D 158, (1973).
State v. Olive, 515 P2d 668, (1973).
State v. Phelps, 493 P2d 1059, (1978).
State v. Renfro, 56 Hawaii 501, (1975).
State v. Smith, 610 P2d 869, (1980).
Stichting Institute of Medical Marijuana, *S.I.M.M. Debunks 13 Marijuana Myths*, P.O. 2008, 3000 C.A. Rotterdam.
Sturdivant v. State, 439 So 2d 184, (1983).
Taxation of Marihuana Hearings, *House of Representatives*, 75th Congress, 1st Session, (1937).
Tracy v. State, 240 So 2d 847, (1970).
United States v. Thorne, 325 A2d 764, (1974).
Walker v. State, 261 Ga 739, (1991).
Watkins v. State, 701 So 2d 592, (1997).
Weinreb, Lloyd, L., *Criminal Process: Cases, Comment, Questions*, 6th Ed., (1998).
Winters v. State, 545 P2d 786, (1976).
Wright v. State, 236 So 2d 408, (1970).
21 USCS § 844

Appendix

The Marihuana Tax Act of 1937

To impose an occupational excise tax upon certain dealers in marihuana, to impose a transfer tax upon certain dealings in marihuana, and to safeguard the revenue therefrom by registry and recording.

Be it enacted by the Senate and House of Representatives of the United States of America in Congress assembled, That when used in this Act—

(a) The term "person" means an individual, a partnership, trust, association, company, or corporation and includes an officer or employee of a partnership, who, as such officer, employee, or member, is under a duty to perform any act in respect of which any violation of this Act occurs.

(b) The term "marihuana" means all parts of the plant Cannabis sativa L., whether growing or not; the seeds thereof; the resin extracted from any part of such plant; and every compound, manufacture, salt, derivative, mixture, or preparation of such plant, its seeds, or resin; but shall not include the mature stalks of such plant, fiber produced from such stalks, oil or cake made from the seeds of such plant, any other compound, manufacture, salt, derivative, mixture, or preparation of such mature stalks (except the resin extracted therefrom), fiber, oil, or cake, or the sterilized seed of such plant which is incapable of germination.

(c) The term "producer" means any person who (1) plants, cultivates, or in any way facilitates the natural growth of marihuana; or (2) harvest and transfers or makes use of marihuana.

(d) The term "Secretary" means the Secretary of the Treasury and the term "collector" means collector of internal revenue.

(e) The term "transfer" or "transferred" means any type of disposition resulting in a change of possession but shall not include a transfer to a common carrier for the purpose of transporting marihuana.

SEC. 2. (a) Every person who imports, manufactures, produces, compounds, sells, deals in, dispenses, prescribes, administers, or gives away marihuana shall (1) within fifteen days after the effective date of this Act, or (2) before engaging after the expiration of such fifteen-day period in any of the above-mentioned activities, and (3) thereafter, on or before July 1 of each year, pay the following special taxes respectively:

(1) Importers, manufacturers, and compounders of marihuana, $24 per year.

(2) Producers of marihuana (except those included within subdivision (4) of this subsection), $1 per year, or fraction thereof, during which they engage in such activity.

(3) Physicians, dentists, veterinary surgeons, and other practitioners who distribute, dispense, give away, administer, or prescribe marihuana to patients upon whom they in the course of their professional practice are in attendance, $1 per year or fraction thereof during which they engage in any of such activities.

(4) Any person not registered as an importer, manufacturer, producer, or compounder who obtains and uses marihuana in a laboratory for the purpose of research, instruction, or analysis, or who produces marihuana for any such purpose, $1 per year, or fraction thereof, during which he engages in such activities.

(5) Any person who is not a physician, dentist, veterinary surgeon, or other practitioner and who deals in, dispenses, or gives away marihuana, $3 per year: *Provided*, That any person who has registered and paid the special tax as an importer, manufacturer, compounder, or producer, as required by subdivisions (1) and (2) of this subsection, may deal in, dispense, or give away marihuana imported, manufactured, compounded, or produced by him without further payment of the tax imposed by this section.

(b) Where a tax under subdivision (1) or (5) is payable on July 1 of any year it shall be computed for one year; where any such tax is payable on any other day it shall be computed proportionately from the first day of the month in which the liability for the tax accrued to the following July 1.

(c) In the event that any person subject to a tax imposed by this section engages in any of the activities enumerated in subsection (a) of this section at more than one place, such person shall pay the tax with respect to each such place.

(d) Except as otherwise provided, whenever more than one of the activities enumerated in subsection (a) of this section is carried on by the same person at the same time, such person shall pay the tax for each such activity, according to the respective rates prescribed.

(e) Any person subject to the tax imposed by this section shall, upon payment of such tax, register his name or style and his place or places of business with the collector of the district in which such place or places of business are located.

(f) Collectors are authorized to furnish, upon written request, to any person a certified copy of the names of any or all persons who may be listed in their respective collection districts as special tax-payers under this section, upon payment of a fee of $1 for each one hundred of such names or fraction thereof upon such copy so requested.

SEC. 3. (a) No employee of any person who has paid the special tax and registered, as required by section 2 of this Act, acting within the scope of his employment, shall be required to register and pay such special tax.

(b) An officer or employee of the United States, any State, Territory, the District of Columbia, or insular possession, or political subdivision, who, in the exercise of his official duties, engages in any of the activities enumerated in section 2 of this Act shall not be required to register or pay the special tax, but his right to this exemption shall be evidenced in such manner as the Secretary may by regulations prescribe.

SEC. 4. (a) It shall be unlawful for any person required to register and pay the special tax under the provisions of section 2 to import, manufacture, produce, compound, sell, deal in, dispense, distribute, prescribe, administer, or give away marihuana without having so registered and paid such tax.

(b) In any suit or proceeding to enforce the liability imposed by this section or section 2, if proof is made that marihuana was at any time growing upon land under the control of the defendant, such proof shall be presumptive evidence that at such time the defendant was a producer and liable under this section as well as under section 2.

SEC. 5. It shall be unlawful for any person who shall not have paid the special tax and registered, as required by section 2, to send, ship, carry, transport, or deliver any marihuana within any Territory, the District of Columbia, or any insular possession, or from an State, Territory, the District of Columbia, any insular possession of the United States, or the Canal Zone, into any other State, Territory, the District of Columbia, or insular possession of the United States: *Provided*, That nothing contained in this section shall apply to any common carrier engaged in transporting marihuana; or to any employment; or to any person who shall deliver marihuana which has been prescribed or dispensed by a physician, dentist, veterinary surgeon, or other practitioner registered under section 2, who has been employed to prescribe for the particular patient receiving such marihuana; or to any United States, State, county, municipal, District, Territorial, or insular officer or official acting within the scope of his official duties.

SEC. 6. (a) It shall be unlawful for any person, whether or not required to pay a special tax and register under section 2, to transfer marihuana, except in pursuance of a written order of the person to whom such marihuana is transferred, on a form to be issued in blank for that purpose by the Secretary.

(b) Subject to such regulations as the Secretary may prescribe, nothing contained in this section shall apply—

(1) To a transfer of marihuana to a patient by a physician, dentist, veterinary surgeon, or other practitioner registered under section 2, in the course of his professional practice only: *Provided*, That such physician, dentist, veterinary surgeon, or other practitioner shall keep a record of all such marihuana transferred, showing the amount transferred and the name and address of the patient to whom such marihuana is transferred, and such record shall be kept for a period of two years from the date of the transfer of such marihuana, and subject to inspection as provided in section 11.

(2) To a transfer of marihuana, made in good faith by a dealer to a consumer under and in pursuance of a written prescription issued by a physician, dentist, veterinary surgeon, or other practitioner registered under section 2: *Provided*, That such prescription shall be dated as of the day on which signed and shall be signed by the physician, dentist, veterinary surgeon, or other practitioner who issues the same: *Provided further*, That such dealer shall preserve such prescription for a period of two years from the day on which such prescription is filled so as to be readily accessible for inspection by the officers agents, employees, and officials mentioned in section 11.

(3) To the sale, exportation, shipment, or delivery of marihuana by any person within the United States, any Territory, the District of Columbia, or any of the insular possessions of the United States, to any person in any foreign country regulating the entry of marihuana, if such sale,

shipment, or delivery of marihuana is made in accordance with such regulations for importation into such foreign country as are prescribed by such foreign country, such regulations to be promulgated from time to time by the Secretary of State of the United States.

(4) To a transfer of marihuana to any officer or employee of the United States Government or of any State, Territorial, District, county, or municipal or insular government lawfully engaged in making purchases thereof for the various departments of the Army and Navy, the Public Health Service, and for Government, State, Territorial, District, county, or municipal or insular hospitals or prisons.

(5) To a transfer of any seeds of the plant Cannabis sativa L. to any person registered under section 2.

(c) The Secretary shall cause suitable forms to be prepared for the purposes before mentioned and shall cause them to be distributed to collectors for sale. The price at which such forms shall be sold by said collectors shall be fixed by the Secretary, but shall not exceed 2 cents each. Whenever any collector shall sell any of such forms he shall cause the date of sale, the name and address of the purchaser, and the amount of marihuana ordered to be plainly written or stamped thereon before delivering the same.

(d) Each such order form sold by a collector shall be prepared by him and shall include an original and two copies, any of which shall be admissible in evidence as an original. The original and one copy shall be given by the collector to the purchaser thereof. The original shall in turn be given by the purchaser thereof to him and shall be preserved by such person for a period of two years so as to be readily accessible for inspection by any officer, agent, or employee mentioned in section 11. The second copy shall be preserved in the records of the collector.

SEC. 7. (a) There shall be levied, collected, and paid upon all transfers of marihuana which are required by section 6 to be carried out in pursuance of written order forms taxes at the following rates:

(1) Upon each transfer to any person who has paid the special tax and registered under section 2 to this Act, $1 per ounce of marihuana or fraction thereof.

(2) Upon each transfer to any person who has not paid the special tax and registered under section 2 of this Act, $100 per ounce of marihuana or fraction thereof.

(b) Such tax shall be paid by the transferee at the time of securing each order from and shall be in addition to the price of such form.

Such transferee shall be liable for the tax imposed by this section but in the event that the transfer is made in violation of section 6 without an order form and without payment of the transfer tax imposed by this section, the transferor shall also be liable for such tax.

(c) Payment of the tax herein provided shall be represented by appropriate stamps to be provided by the Secretary and said stamps shall be affixed by the collector or his representative to the original order form.

(d) All provisions of law relating to the engraving, issuance, sale, accountability, cancellation, and destruction of tax-paid stamps provided for in the internal-revenue laws shall, insofar as applicable and not inconsistent with this Act, be extended and made to apply to stamps provided for in this section.

(e) All provisions of law (including penalties) applicable in respect of the taxes imposed by the Act of December 17, 1914 (38 Stat. 785; U.S.C., 1934 ed., title 26, secs. 1040-1061, 1383-1391), as amended, shall, insofar as not inconsistent with this Act, be applicable in respect of the taxes imposed by this Act.

SEC. 8. (a) It shall be unlawful for any person who is a transferee required to pay the transfer tax imposed by section 7 to acquire or otherwise obtain any marihuana without having paid such tax; and proof that any person shall have had in his possession any marihuana and shall have failed, after reasonable notice and demand by the collector, to produce the order form required by section 6 to by retained by him, shall be presumptive evidence of guilty under this section and of liability for the tax imposed by section 7.

(b) No liability shall be imposed by virtue of this section upon any duly authorized officer of the Treasury Department engaged in any State, or Territory, or of any political subdivision thereof, or the District of Columbia, or of any insular possession of the United States, who shall be engaged in the enforcement of any law or municipal ordinance dealing with the production, sale, prescribing, dispensing, dealing in, or distributing of marihuana.

SEC. 9. (a) Any marihuana which has been imported, manufacture, compounded, transferred, or produced in violation of any of the provisions of this Act shall be subject to seizure and forfeiture and, except as inconsistent with the provisions of this Act, all the provisions of internal-revenue laws relating to searches, seizures, and forfeitures are extended to include marihuana.

(b) Any marihuana which may be seized by the United States Government from any person or persons charged with any violation of this Act shall upon conviction of the person or persons from whom seized by confiscated by and forfeited to the United States.

(c) Any marihuana seized or coming into the possession of the United States in the enforcement of this Act, the owner or owners of which are unknown, shall be confiscated by and forfeited to the United States.

(d) The Secretary is hereby directed to destroy any marihuana confiscated by and forfeited to the United States under this section or to deliver such marihuana to any department, bureau, or other agency of the United States Government, upon proper application therefore under such regulations as may be prescribed by the Secretary.

SEC. 10. (a) Every person liable to any tax imposed by this Act shall keep such books and records, render under oath such statements, make such returns, and comply with such rules and regulations as the Secretary may from time to time prescribe.

(b) Any person who shall be registered under the provisions of section 2 in any internal-revenue district shall, whenever required so to do by the collector of the district, render to the collector a true and correct statement or return, verified by affidavits, setting for the quantity of marihuana received or harvested by him during such period immediately preceding the demand of the collector, not exceeding three months, as the said collector may fix and determine. If such person is not solely a producer, he shall set forth in such statement or return the names of the persons from whom said marihuana was received, the quantity in each instance received from such persons, and the date when received.

SEC. 11. The order forms and copies thereof and the prescriptions and records required to be preserved under the provisions of section 6, and the statements or returns filed in the office of the collector of the district under the provisions of section 10 (b) shall be open to inspection by officers, agents, and employees of the Treasury Department duly authorized for that purpose, and such officers of any State, or Territory, or of any political subdivision thereof, or the District of Columbia, or of any insular possession of the United States as shall be charged with the enforcement of any law or municipal ordinance regulating the production, sale, prescribing, dispensing, dealing in, or distributing of marihuana. Each collector shall be authorized to furnish, upon written request, copies of any of the said statements or returns filed in his office to any of such officials of any

State or territory, or political subdivision thereof, or the District of Columbia, or any insular possession of the United States as shall be entitled to inspect the said statements or returns filed in the office of the said collector, upon the payment of a fee of $1 for each 100 words or fraction thereof in the copy or copies so requested.

SEC. 12. Any person who is convicted of a violation of any provision of this Act shall be fined not more than $2,000 or imprisoned not more than five years, or both, in the discretion of the court.

SEC. 13. It shall not be necessary to negative any exemption set forth in this Act in any complaint, information, indictment, or other writ or proceeding laid or brought under this Act and the burden of proof of any such exemption shall be upon the defendant. In the absence of the production of evidence by the defendant that he has complied with the provisions of section 2 relating to registration or that he has complied with the provisions of section 6 relating to order forms, he shall be presumed not to have complied with such provisions of such sections, as the case may be.

SEC. 14. The Secretary is authorized to make, prescribe, and publish all necessary rules and regulations for carrying out the provisions of this Act and to confer or impose any of the rights, privileges, powers, and duties conferred or imposed upon him by this Act upon such officers or employees of the Treasury Department as he shall designate or appoint.

SEC. 15. The provisions of this Act shall apply to the several States, the District of Columbia, the Territory of Alaska, the Territory of Hawaii, and the insular possession of the United States, except the Philippine Islands. In Puerto Rico the administration of this Act, the collection of the special taxes and transfer taxes, and the issuance of the order forms provided for in section 6 shall be performed by the appropriate internal-revenue officers of that government, and all revenues collected under this Act in Puerto Rico shall accrue intact to the general government thereof. The President is hereby authorized and directed to issue such Executive orders as will carry into effect in the Virgin Islands the intent and purpose of this Act by providing for the registration with appropriate officers and the imposition of the special and transfer taxes upon all persons in the Virgin Islands who import, manufacture, produce, compound, sell, deal in, dispense, prescribe, administer, or give away marihuana.

SEC. 16. If any provision of this Act or the application thereof to any person or circumstances is held invalid, the reminder of the Act and the application of such provision to other persons or circumstances shall not be affected thereby.

SEC. 17. This Act shall take effect on the first day of the second month after the month during which it is enacted.

SEC. 18. This Act may be cited as the "Marihuana Tax Act of 1937."

Approved, August 2, 1937.

Notes

[1] Abel at 189.
[2] Grinspoon at 10.
[3] Id.
[4] Id.
[5] Solomon at xiv.
[6] Id. at 80.
[7] Id. at 84.
[8] Grinspoon at 12.
[9] Id. at 14.
[10] Bonnie and Whitebread at 1010.
[11] Grinspoon at 16.
[12] Bonnie and Whitebread at 990.
[13] High Times at 30.
[14] Grinspoon at 20.
[15] High Times at 31.
[16] Bonnie and Whitebread at 1037.
[17] Solomon at xxiii.
[18] Anslinger.
[19] Id.
[20] Abel at 189.
[21] Solomon at xxiv.
[22] Anslinger.
[23] Solomon at xxiv.
[24] Id.
[25] Id.
[26] Grinspoon at 27.
[27] Solomon at xxv.
[28] National Commission on Marihuana at 8.
[29] Bonnie and Whitebread at 1049.
[30] Grinspoon at 17.

[31] Bonnie and Whitebread at 1052.
[32] Abel at 210.
[33] Id. at 215.
[34] Id. at 222.
[35] Anslinger.
[36] Abel at 226.
[37] Id. at 225.
[38] Id. at 245.
[39] Id. at 230.
[40] Id. at 230.
[41] *Reefer Madness*.
[42] Id.
[43] Id.
[44] Id.
[45] Tax Act Hearings.
[46] Solomon at xiv.
[47] Grinspoon at 339.
[48] Abel at 190.
[49] Id.
[50] Id. at 191.
[51] Id.
[52] Grinspoon at 332.
[53] Id.
[54] Tax Act Hearings.
[55] Id. italics added.
[56] Id. italics added.
[57] High Times at 29.
[58] Grinspoon at 22.
[59] Tax Act Hearings.
[60] Solomon at 93.
[61] Id.
[62] Abel at 214.
[63] Grinspoon at 16.
[64] Id.
[65] Bonnie and Whitebread at 971.
[66] Id. at 1054.
[67] Tax Act Hearings.
[68] Id.

[69] Id.
[70] Id.
[71] Id.
[72] Id.
[73] Id.
[74] Id.
[75] Id.
[76] Id.
[77] Grinspoon at 22.
[78] Tax Act Hearings.
[79] Id.
[80] Id.
[81] Id.
[82] Id.
[83] Id.
[84] Id.
[85] Bonnie and Whitehead at 1054.
[86] Tax Act Hearings.
[87] Id.
[88] Id.
[89] Id.
[90] Id.
[91] Bonnie and Whitebread at 1062.
[92] Tax Act.
[93] Id.
[94] Id.
[95] Id.
[96] Id.
[97] Id.
[98] Id.
[99] Id.
[100] Id.
[101] Id.
[102] Id.
[103] Id.
[104] Id.
[105] Id.
[106] Id.

[107] Id.
[108] Bonnie and Whitebread at 1063.
[109] Grinspoon at 339.
[110] Id. at 21.
[111] Drug War Facts at 26.
[112] Grinspoon at 322.
[113] Id. at 12.
[114] DEA Congressional Testimony.
[115] Drug War Facts at 1.
[116] Id.
[117] Id. at 37.
[118] Id. at 38.
[119] Id. at 39.
[120] Id.
[121] National Commission on Marihuana at 145.
[122] National Commission on Marihuana at 140.
[123] DEA Congressional Testimony.
[124] Id.
[125] National Commission on Marihuana at 128.
[126] DEA Congressional Testimony.
[127] Id.
[128] Drug War Facts at 35.
[129] DEA Congressional Testimony.
[130] Drug War Facts at 35.
[131] DEA Congressional Testimony.
[132] *Ravin.*
[133] Grinspoon at 8.
[134] National Commission on Marihuana at 152.
[135] Drug War Facts at 35.
[136] Huffman.
[137] Stichting Institute of Medical Marijuana.
[138] Drug Facts at 5.
[139] Id.
[140] DEA Congressional Testimony.
[141] Id.
[142] Id.
[143] Anslinger.
[144] "Toward Legalization?" December 2, 1996; "Republicans, White House

unite to fight new drug laws," December 2, 1996; "Clinton may oppose medical use of illicit drugs," November 29, 1996; "Law enforcement officials fear marijuana law fallout," November 16, 1996; "California OK's Marijuana For Medicinal Use," November 5, 1996; "Marijuana proponents relish victory," November 6, 1996; "California Could Legalize Pot in Bumper Crop of Propositions," November 3, 1996; "Mexico making headway in war against drugs," September 18, 1997; "Weed Wars," December 30, 1996; "San Francisco club raid re-ignites conflict over legalized marijuana," April 22, 1997; "No Deal on Medical Marijuana," February 10, 1997; "Saying No To Drugs," December 30, 1996; "Singing the praises of pot on 'Hempilation 2,'" November 20, 1998; "Study casts doubt on marijuana's effectiveness as glaucoma treatment," November 13, 1998; "City of San Francisco may get into medical pot business," May 30, 1998; "Medical marijuana grower slapped with stiff sentence," August 7, 1999; "Drug Crazy," February 4, 1999; "New York baggage claim: $1 Million in Marijuana," January 10, 1999; "Survey of teens shows reduction of drug use," December 18, 1998; "Hawaii governor signs medical marijuana bill," June 14, 2000; "Main sheriff proposes seized pot be used for medicinal purposes," May 12, 2000; "Multination drug sweep nets 2,331 arrests," March 29, 2000; "Bel Air pot grower sentenced to prison," March 27, 2000; "Links found between marijuana and vision," December 7, 1999; "Medical marijuana rules criticized," November 30, 1999; "Teen-age drug use down, anti-drug group's survey finds," November 22, 1999. (CNN).

[145] Id.
[146] Id.
[147] Id.
[148] Id.
[149] Id.
[150] Id.
[151] *Mountain Bike.*
[152] SPRINT.
[153] See the A.L.R. under *marijuana.*
[154] *Ravin.*
[155] Id.
[156] Id.
[157] *State v. Kantner.*
[158] *Griswold* in dissent by Black.
[159] Law Review Articles—Soler, Of Cannabis and the Courts: A Critical

Examination of Constitution Challenges to Statutory Marijuana Prohibitions. 6 Conn L Rev. 601, 1974, Greenstein & Di Bianco, Marijuana Laws—A Crime Against Humanity. 48 Notre Dame Lawyer 314, December 1972, Comment—Marijuana Possession and the California Constitutional Prohibition of Cruel or Unusual Punishment. 21 UCLA L Rev. 1136, April 1974, Comment—Ravin v. State: A Case for Privacy and Possession of Pot. 5 UCLA-Alaska L Rev 178, fall, 1975, Bonnie & Whitebread, The Forbidden Fruit and the Tree of Knowledge: An Inquiry Into the Legal History of American Marijuana Prohibition. 56 Va. L Rev. 971, October 1970; UNITED STATES—21 USCS § 844(a). See § 2[b], Clark v. Craven (1971, CA 9 Cal) 437 F2d 1202-§ 5[a], Louisiana Affiliate of Nat. Organization for Reform of Marijuana Laws (NORML) v. Guste (1974, ED La) 380 F. Supp 404-§§ 5[b], 6, 8, Rogers v. Estelle (1978, CA 5 Tex) 571 F2d 1381, Stanley v. Georgia (1969) 394 US 557, State v. Leigh (1978) 46 USLW 2425, United States Supreme Court in Stanley v. Georgia (1969) 394 US 557, Wolkind v. Selph (1979) 473 F. Supp. 675, Wright v. Edwards (1972) 343 F Supp. 792; ALABAMA—Cain v. State (1990) 830 P2d 435, Eighth Amendment. Dickerson v. State (1982) 414 So 2d 998, Haynes v. State (1975) 312 So 2d 406, Sturdivant v. State (1983) 439 So 2d 184; ALASKA—Allam v. State (992) 830 P2d 435, Ravin v. State (1975) 537 P2d 494; ARIZONA—State v. Murphy (1977) 570 P2d 1070, CALIFORNIA—People v. Aguiar (1968) 257 Cal App. 2d 597, People v. Bloom (1969) 270 Cal App 2d 731,People v. Foster (1968) 260 Cal App 2d 84, People v. Glaser (1965) 238 Cal App 2d 819, People v. Irvin (1968) 264 Cal App 2d 747, People v. Oatis (1968) 264 Cal App 2d 324, People v. Oliver (1944) 66 Cal App 2d 431, People v. Tharp (1969) 272 Cal App 2d 268, People v. Widener (1963) 220 Cal App 2d 826, People v. Trippet (1997) 56 Cal App 4th 1532; COLORADO—Normand v. People (1968) 440 P2d 282, People v. McKenzie (1969) 458 P2d 232, People v. Velasquez (1983) 666 P2d 567; DELAWARE—Kreisher v. State (1974) 319 A2d 31; DISTRICT OF COLUMBIA—United States v. Thorne (1974) 325 A2d 764; FLORIDA—Albo V. State (1980) 379 So 2d 648, Borras v. State (1969) 229 So 2d 244, Cuevas v. State (1969) 279 So 2d 817, Fotianos v. State (1976) 329 So 2d 397, Hamilton v. State (1978) 366 So 2d 8, Laird v. State (1977) 342 So 2d 962, Maisler v. State (1982) 425 So 2d 107, Tracy v. State (1970) 240 So 2d 847, Watkins v. State (1997) 701 So 2d 592; GEORGIA—Blincoe v. State (1974) 231 Ga 886, Walker v. State (1991) 261 Ga 739; HAWAII—State v. Baker (1975) 56 Hawaii 271, State v. Kantner (1972) 53 Hawaii 327, State v. Renfro (1975) 56 Hawaii 501; IDAHO—State

v. Kelly (1984) 106 Idaho 268, State v. Kincaid (1977) 98 Idaho 440; ILLINOIS—Illinois Norml, Inc. v. Scott (1978) 66 Ill App 3d 633, People v. Brisco (1979) 78 Ill App 3d 282, People v. Campbell (1974) 16 Ill App 3d 851, People v. Downing (1976) 37 Ill App 3d 297, People v. Kline (1974) 16 Ill App 3d 1017, People v. Mayberry (1976) 63 Ill App 2d 1, People v. McCaffrey (1975) 29 Ill App 3d 1088, People v. Rhoades (1979) 74 Ill App 3d 247, People v. Hesse (1974) 18 Ill App 3d 669; IOWA—State v. Lange (1994) 529 NW2d 615, State v. Leins (1975) 234 NW2d 645; KANSAS—State v. McBride (1998) 24 Kan. App 2d 909; LOUISIANA—State v. Bonoa (1931) 136 So 15, State v. Chrisman (1978) 364 So 2d 906, State v. Harian (1990) 556 So 2d 256; MASSACHUSETTS—Commonwealth v. Leis (1969) 243 NE2d 898, Marcoux v. Atty. Gen. (1978) 375 NE2d 688; MICHIGAN—People v. Pearson (1987) 403 NW2d 498, People v. Riddle (1975) 237 NW2d 491, People v. Shackelford (1985) 379 NW2d 487, People v. Sinclair (1972) 194 NW2d 878, People v. Waxman (1972) 199 NW2d 884, People v. Williams (1984) 355 NW2d 268; MISSISSIPPI—Wright v. State (1970) 236 So 2d 408; NEBRASKA—State v. Infante (1977) 260 NW2d 323, State v. Kells (1977) 259 NW2d 19, State v. Neal (1971) 191 NW2d 458; NEW JERSEY—State v. Nugent (1973) 312 a2D 158; NEW MEXICO—State v. Olive (1973) 515 P2d 668; NEW YORK—People v. Fillhart (1978) 403 NYS2d 642, People v. Nissen (1979) 412 NYS2d 999, People v. Perez (1967) 289 NYS2d 450, People v. Young (1974) 361 NYS2d 762; NORTH CAROLINA—State v. Kaplan (1974) 209 se2D 325; OKLAHOMA—Brantley v. State (1976) 548 P2d 675, Cavaness v. State (1978) 581 P2d 475, Crow v. State (1976) 551 P2d 279, Winters v. State (1976) 545 P2d 786; OREGON—State v. Phelps (1978) 493 P2d 1059; RHODE ISLAND—State v. Beck (1974) 329 A2d 190; TEXAS—Arredondo v. State (1959) 324 SW2d 217, Broom v. State (1970) 463 SW2d 220, Martinez v. State (1963) 373 SW2d 246, Miller v. State (1970) 458 SW2d 680; WASHINGTON—State v. Anderson (1976) 558 P2d 307, State v. Dickamore (1979) 592 P2d 681, State v. Gerry (1979) 595 P2d 49, State v. Smith (1980) 610 P2d 869; WEST VIRGINIA—State ex rel. Scott v. Conaty (1972) 187 SE2d 119. (ALR)

[160] Headlines have reported rulings on both sides of the equation. One CNN story reported, "Judge bans government from pursuing doctors who recommend marijuana for treatment." While another CNN story reported, "Appeals court rules against California marijuana clubs."

[161] *Draper v. United States.*

[162] *Illinois v. Gates.*
[163] Id.
[164] *Florida v. Bostick.*
[165] Id. italics added.
[166] Id.
[167] Id.
[168] *Rochin v. California.*
[169] Id.
[170] Weinreb at 360.
[171] Dukeminier at 376.
[172] 21 USCS §844.
[173] Grinspoon at 323.
[174] Id.
[175] Put simply, a fully informed adult has the right to do whatever he or she pleases provided no one else is harmed by their conduct.